ACTIVITY BANK

Self-Esteem

Christine Moorcroft

Contents

How to use this book ... 3

Introduction ... 3

Activity

1	I can do it!	4
2	This is me!	6
3	Self-respect	8
4	Mirror image	10
5	The same but different	12
6	Body language	14
7	Face, hands and body	16
8	Your values	18
9	Values and actions	20
10	Feedback	22
11	Not again!	24
12	Taking charge	26
13	On the surface?	28
14	No panic!	30
15	Getting angry	32
16	Feeling and thinking	34
17	Stressed out	36
18	Stress busters	38
19	Sad or depressed?	40
20	Danger – eating disorders	42
21	Emotions and eating	44
22	Help	46
	Skills matrix	48

© 2002 Folens Limited, on behalf of the author.

United Kingdom: Folens Publishers, Apex Business Centre, Boscombe Road, Dunstable, LU5 4RL.
Email: folens@folens.com

Ireland: Folens Publishers, Greenhills Road, Tallaght, Dublin 24.
Email: info@folens.ie

Poland: JUKA, ul. Renesansowa 38, Warsaw 01-905.

Folens allows photocopying of pages marked 'copiable page' for educational use, providing that this use is within the confines of the purchasing institution. Copiable pages should not be declared in any return in respect of any photocopying licence.

Folens publications are protected by international copyright laws. All rights are reserved. The copyright of all materials in this publication, except where otherwise stated, remains the property of the publisher and author. No part of this publication may be reproduced, stored in a retrieval system, or transmitted, in any form or by any means, for whatever purpose, without the written permission of Folens Limited.

Christine Moorcroft hereby asserts her moral right to be identified as the author of this work in accordance with the Copyright, Designs and Patents Act 1988.

Editor: Sue Harmes
Layout artist: Suzanne Ward
Cover design: Martin Cross
Illustrations: Pauline King (Linda Rogers Associates)

First published 2002 by Folens Limited.

Every effort has been made to trace the copyright holders of material used in this publication. If any copyright holder has been overlooked, we should be pleased to make any necessary arrangements.

British Library Cataloguing in Publication Data. A catalogue record for this publication is available from the British Library.
ISBN 184303 152-3

How to use this book

There are 22 activities contained within this book. Each one has a teacher instruction page and a pupil activity page. The activities can be completed in short time slots or extended into longer periods, depending on the length of time you have available. They can also be differentiated to suit the needs of less able pupils. The activities can be presented in any order, unless otherwise stated; they have been designed to stand alone, or to supplement other programmes of study. There is a wide selection of teaching strategies, techniques and activities that teachers can use as a source of ideas. A matrix on page 48 provides a useful summary of – and reference to – the skills that pupils will learn through the activities.

Most of the activities in this book need few materials or resources other than copies of the activity sheet, paper and pens. They are designed to keep the teacher's workload to a minimum, beyond planning how each activity will be carried out in the classroom. Most are designed so that pupils can work individually, in pairs or in small groups, depending on the teacher's preference. A balance is recommended of whole class, small group and individual work, with plenty of opportunity for the pupils to express their views, to listen and try to understand the views of others and to develop communication and social skills, plus knowledge of citizenship. Teachers will need to be aware and sensitive to the pupils' cultural and religious backgrounds when planning lessons, and to be willing to handle values and controversial issues in the classroom.

The aims and expected outcomes of each activity are clearly indicated and the format for all activities is consistent to enable you quickly to feel comfortable and familiar with the style. All the information a teacher will need is given in this book, or can be found on websites listed in the book, so that the teacher will be confident in presenting the lessons, and will be able to answer most of the questions that may arise.

Introduction

Activity Bank Self-Esteem provides 22 photocopiable activities (each accompanied by notes for teachers) to support the teaching of the National Curriculum Non-statutory Guidelines for Personal, Social and Health Education at Key Stages 3 and 4 and the new scheme of work for Citizenship.

Self-esteem is a crucial aspect of personal, social and health education, since research has shown that the greater the pupils' self-esteem, the more positive their approach to issues such as taking responsibility for their own actions, developing a healthy lifestyle and resisting peer pressure to take part in activities they know to be unwise.

The book helps pupils to develop the confidence to act on their knowledge of what is right or wrong, healthy or unhealthy, sensible or unwise and considerate or inconsiderate. It helps them to take responsibility for their own behaviour and its consequences, to develop and make the most of their own abilities, skills and personal qualities, to acknowledge any problems they have and to solve those they can, and to recognise situations in which they need to seek help (and know where to find it).

Activity Bank Self-Esteem focuses on the aspects of the Guidelines for Personal, Social and Health Education that are connected with the development of self-esteem (see the skills matrix on page 48).

It also contributes to the development of key cross-curricular skills including thinking skills, abilities and attitudes: analysing/interpreting, asserting, developing awareness, collating, communicating, comparing, cooperating, debating and discussing, making decisions, empathising, evaluating, expressing beliefs, opinions and ideas, using ICT, developing identity, self-esteem and imagination, investigating, using knowledge, listening, developing perception and presentation, prioritising, problem-solving, respecting (oneself and others), responsibility and understanding.

Activity 1 – Teacher's notes

I can do it!

Tackling negative thoughts

AIM

To help pupils to develop a positive approach to challenges.

Teaching Points

- Self-confidence is not necessarily linked to ability, but to a person's perceptions of his or her ability to achieve an aim or carry out a task.
- Unrealistic expectations can damage self-confidence.
- Self-confidence can be built up through recognising the negative factors that diminish it and turning them into positive factors by identifying achievements, skills and qualities.
- Self-confidence can be developed by setting achievable (but worthwhile) targets and believing that they can be met.

USING THE ACTIVITY SHEET

The focus of the activity is to encourage pupils to develop self-confidence through tackling negative thoughts.

Step 1 Tell the class that the purpose of the lesson is to identify the self-doubts that stop people achieving or doing things because they 'think they can't'. Tell them about someone (anonymous) who could not face something because of not feeling able to do it well: for example, a pupil staying away from school to avoid giving a talk to the class, or tearing up every attempt at a painting. Ask the pupils to think of other situations that people might not feel able to face.

Step 2 Ask the pupils to complete the first part of the activity sheet. Invite them to share their answers. Record their responses on a board or overhead transparency, keeping a tally of the number of times any of them is repeated. Ask the pupils why these particular activities might evoke the response 'I can't'.

Step 3 Ask the pupils to complete the second part of the activity individually. You could give them a time limit for this and tell them that they should begin a group discussion of their ideas once the time limit is reached.

Step 4 Invite feedback about the negative thoughts that stop people achieving, and the ways in which they would tackle these thoughts. Emphasise positive thinking: for example, if people think they cannot do something well, they could bring to mind what they *can* do and tell themselves they can improve. Point out that achieving success might require several attempts; they will need to practise and notice any improvements they make, however small. Ask the pupils to complete the final part of the activity.

Extension Activities

- The pupils could make a note of something about which they have not felt confident, and identify the negative thoughts that caused this. With a friend they could work on positive thoughts – writing down anything they *can* do that will help.
- Pupils could write a ten-point plan for ways of developing self-confidence.

Outcomes

- Developing self-confidence.
- Developing strategies to overcome negative feelings.

Activity Sheet 1

I can do it!

1. Sometimes people feel as if they cannot do something. They do not feel confident. Write an example of a situation where someone might lack confidence, such as starting a new school.

   _____

2. In the 'thought bubbles', write some of the negative thoughts this person might have.

3. In your group, discuss what you have written and think of ways in which to turn each negative thought into a positive thought. Write your ideas in the flashes.

© Folens (copiable page)   ACTIVITY BANK: *Self-Esteem*

Activity 2 – Teacher's notes

This is me!

Being aware of, and drawing on, one's own skills, talents and qualities

AIM

To develop pupils' awareness of their own skills, talents and qualities, so that they can draw on them to meet challenges.

Teaching Points

- Everyone has a unique combination of skills, talents and qualities that make him or her an individual.
- Awareness of, and belief in, these skills, talents and qualities leads to high self-esteem.
- If people believe in their own abilities they can use them in facing challenges.
- It can be difficult or embarrassing to talk about what we are good at, but it is a useful skill, especially in convincing others that we can cope with a task (for example in a job interview).
- Talking about our skills, talents and qualities is not boasting; we should be realistic and be prepared to give examples to support what we say.

USING THE ACTIVITY SHEET

The focus of the activity is to help pupils to identify their own skills, talents and qualities and to present them to others in a convincing way.

Step 1 Tell the pupils that the purpose of the lesson is to develop their awareness of their skills, talents and qualities and to practise talking about them in a convincing, but not boastful, way. You could model how *not* to do this: for example, by looking away from the audience, muttering and using expressions like 'I'm not too bad at … ',
'I might be able to … a bit' and 'I could have been good at … if I'd had the chance'. You could make it humorous. Ask the pupils to comment on what you did wrong.

Step 2 Model the opposite approach: use exaggerated gestures, a loud voice and boastful or even arrogant statements, such as 'I'm brilliant at …', 'I'm a world-class …' or 'You won't find anyone who has better skills than I have in …'. Again, you could make it humorous. Ask the pupils to comment on what you did wrong.

Step 3 Ask the pupils to complete the activity sheet. Invite volunteers to deliver their speech, and ask the others to offer praise and criticism that will help them to improve it.

Step 4 Point out that the pupils can refer to the activity sheet whenever they face a challenge in which they think they might fail. Encourage them to bring to mind their skills, talents and qualities and to use those that are the most appropriate for the situation. Discuss examples from their completed activity sheets.

Extension Activities

- The pupils could make video recordings of their speeches as commercials, watch them and make notes about how to improve them.
- Give the pupils a list of challenging situations and ask them to choose those in which they think they would do best. They could write about how they would tackle them and which skills, talents and qualities they would use.

Outcomes

- Developing the pupils' self-esteem through the recognition of their skills, talents and qualities, and understanding when these can be useful.
- Developing positive approaches to challenges.

Activity Sheet 2

This is me!

1. Look at the skills, talents and qualities in the boxes. Circle the ones you have. In the blank boxes, write some more that apply to you.

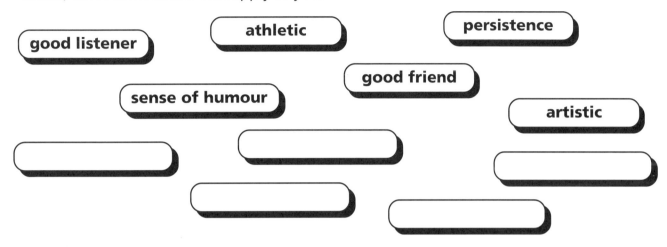

2. Make notes for a 30-second speech with which you can convince someone else of your skills and qualities.

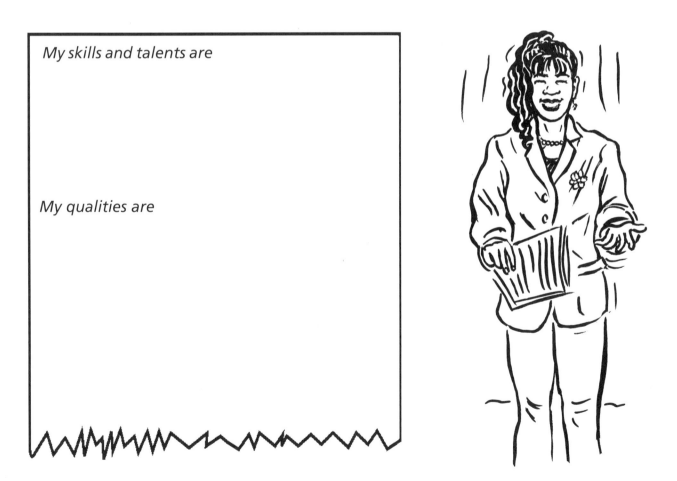

My skills and talents are

My qualities are

3. Write the script for your speech on the back of this sheet; then practise it.

Activity 3 – Teacher's notes

Self-respect

How people show self-respect

AIM

To develop pupils' awareness of the effects of self-respect on their own and other people's behaviour.

Teaching Points

- Self-respect means having values and trying to act in accordance with them.
- Different people have different values: for example, some people value cleanliness and tidiness more than others, some people think it is wrong to eat animals, some people feel they should do whatever they want as long as it does not harm others.
- There are many values that are shared by individuals and communities: for example, the belief that it is wrong to steal, to gossip about others or to dress in particular ways.
- Self-respect includes respecting the values of other people.

USING THE ACTIVITY SHEET

The focus of the activity is to encourage pupils to identify the factors that constitute self-respect.

Step 1 Tell the class that the purpose of the lesson is to consider what is meant by self-respect. Examples of people who demonstrate self-respect might be a pupil who stands up to group pressure to join in with bullying another class member, or a student who decides to spend their summer holiday working in a Romanian orphanage. Ask pupils what they think self-respect means, and write their definitions on a chalkboard, wipe-off board or overhead transparency, separating any that focus on actions or behaviour from those that are merely labels.

Step 2 Ask the pupils to comment on the way in which you have separated their definitions, and draw out the idea of self-respect as something that people can develop and that is shown by what they do. Tell the pupils that the activity sheet asks them to concentrate on what people *do* that shows their self-respect or lack of it. Ask the pupils to complete the first part of the activity sheet, focusing on actions and behaviour.

Step 3 Invite the pupils to share their responses to the first activity with the rest of the class. Encourage them to ask questions that begin, 'If you had self-respect, would you …?' Ask the rest of the class to give answers. Discuss any questions to which the answer is not clear-cut (depending on the person's values).

Step 4 Ask the pupils to complete the activity sheet. Invite feedback and ask them to contribute ideas for completing a list of the ways in which increased self-respect can improve someone's everyday life; focus on what happens, and include examples.

Extension Activities

- As an individual activity, the pupils could evaluate their own self-respect (they need not share the results with anyone else) on a ten-point scale and identify actions they could take to increase it.

Outcomes

- Understanding the factors that contribute to self-respect.
- Developing the pupils' own self-respect.

Activity Sheet 3

Self-respect

Sam shows high self-respect in the way in which he eats healthily.

Gemma shows low self-respect in the way in which she leaves her bedroom untidy.

1. Think about people who have self-respect and those who do not. How do they show this by what they do? Write your ideas in the boxes with annotated drawings if you like.

Someone who has high self-respect	Someone who has low self-respect
Does	Does
Does not	Does not

2. Make notes about how other people might treat the people above.

Someone who has high self-respect	Someone who has little self-respect

© Folens (copiable page)   ACTIVITY BANK: *Self-Esteem*

Activity 4 – Teacher's notes

Mirror image

Self-images and how other people see us

AIM

To develop pupils' awareness of how others see them compared with the images they have of themselves.

Teaching Points

- We do not always see ourselves as others do.
- Our actions might not have the effects on others that we intend.
- Comments are helpful when they are supported by examples of behaviour, for example, 'When you played at dodging the traffic in the High Street; this might make others think you need to show off', rather than 'You are a show-off.'
- It is important to express negative points tactfully and in a way that shows understanding and wanting to help the person.

USING THE ACTIVITY SHEET

The focus of the activity is to encourage pupils to identify the effects of their behaviour on the ways in which other people respond to them.

Step 1 Tell the class that the purpose of the lesson is to help them to become aware of the image they present to other people and how it affects people's responses. They will also learn how to help their friends in this process. Tell them that they are going to begin by describing how they see themselves.

Step 2 Ask the pupils to complete the first 'mirror'. After they have done so, invite any who are willing to share their responses, or ask them to read through their responses and look for any that are descriptive (for example, 'I am artistic' or 'I am useless at sport') and encourage pupils to express them as actions rather than giving themselves labels: for example, 'I can draw portraits well' or 'I cannot throw a ball well'.

Step 3 Ask the pupils to complete the second mirror, about their friend, in terms of actions rather than labels. Then invite them to compare their own and their friend's versions and to discuss with the friend what they have written.

Step 4 Point out that people often make mistakes about the impressions they give to others because they might not realise what messages their actions convey: for example, someone who wants to appear calm and cool might give the impression of not caring about others. Also discuss the reasons why people might try to create an impression that is different from what they are really like: perhaps they do not like something about themselves.

Extension Activities

- Discuss the similarities and differences between people and the importance of individuality. The pupils could write a statement of something that is important to them, and share their thoughts with a friend.
- The pupils could learn about and write a report on how to understand people through their body language and about the impression their own body language might give. (See Activity 6.)

Outcomes

- Comparison of self-images with those held by other people.
- Ability of pupils to appreciate their own positive qualities.

Activity Sheet 4

Mirror image

1. Fold the page in two on the dotted line.
   In the first mirror, write notes about your 'self-image' (how you appear to yourself).

Fold here

- -

2. Work with a friend you trust. In the mirror below, ask your friend to make notes about your 'image' (how you appear to other people).

© Folens (copiable page)   ACTIVITY BANK: *Self-Esteem*

Activity 5 – Teacher's notes

The same but different

Comparing people's opinions and choice of roles in life

AIM

To develop pupils' respect for other people whose opinions and the way they choose to live are different from their own.

Teaching Points

- Different people respond to similar situations in different ways. These differences can strengthen a group.
- People have different likes, dislikes, opinions and values, and these should be respected.
- The differences among people can arise from differences in personality, culture, beliefs or values.
- People should not be excluded from a group because they do not have the same views or outlooks as the majority.

USING THE ACTIVITY SHEET

The focus of the activity is to encourage the pupils to identify, understand and respect the similarities and differences between themselves and others.

Step 1 Tell the class that the purpose of the lesson is to help them to understand some of their own opinions and those of others. Tell them that the activity begins with a questionnaire and that, if they prefer, they need only share their responses with a friend they trust. Ask them not to write their names on the questionnaires. Point out that there are no 'right' or 'wrong' answers – it is their own views that are important.

Step 2 Ask the pupils to complete the first activity. Ask them if there are any statements with which they think everyone will agree, and to say why; invite any pupils who disagree to explain their responses. Stress again that there are no 'right' or 'wrong' answers – just different answers.

Step 3 Ask the pupils to complete the rest of the activity sheet. Afterwards, ask them if they were surprised at the results of the comparison. Ask them to explain why.

Step 4 Ask the pupils what they learned from the activity. Talk about any strong views they have and the extent to which they have developed an understanding of opposing views held by other people.

Extension Activities

- Ask the pupils to cut off the questionnaire section of the activity sheet. Collect them, number them and redistribute them. Ask the groups to read the questionnaires they have been given and to discuss which people (referring to the numbers on the sheets) would work well together on particular activities, and why.
- With a partner who has an opposite view about something, the pupils could plan and write a discussion of why each view is valid.

Outcomes

- Understanding some of the ways in which people differ, both on a superficial and on a deeper level.
- Development of pupils' respect for views that are opposed to their own.

Activity Sheet 5

The same but different

Read each statement and put any number from 1 to 10 to show how far you agree with it. Put '10' if you agree completely, '1' if you disagree completely.

1	It is important to wear fashionable clothes.	
2	It is important to wear clothes you like even if they are not fashionable.	
3	It is important to keep your belongings tidy.	
4	It is boring to be neat.	
5	I usually lead any group in which I work.	
6	I do not like working in a group led by someone else.	
7	It is important to obey people in authority.	
8	I like to spend time alone.	
9	In discussions I come up with lots of ideas.	
10	In discussions I often act as scribe.	
11	In discussions I often ask questions.	
12	I like to chair discussions.	
13	I like to organise events and group activities.	
14	I prefer someone else to organise things for me.	
15	I want to do well at sports.	
16	I want to do well in exams.	
17	I want to have a lot of money.	
18	I want to become an expert at something.	
19	I want to be famous.	
20	I want to be in charge of people.	

✂--

Discuss the main differences between your answers and those of your friend. What are the most noticeable differences between your answers?

_____

_____

_____

Choose one of the statements and explain your friend's opinion.

_____

_____

_____

© Folens (copiable page)   ACTIVITY BANK: *Self-Esteem*

Activity 6 – Teacher's notes

Body language

The messages given to other people through expressions, gestures and posture

AIM

To develop pupils' awareness of the messages they give to other people through expressions, gestures and posture.

Teaching Points

Optional materials
Pictures of people (these could be cut from magazines or newspapers) showing different facial expressions, gestures and postures. A picture of someone with a tense, rigid facial expression.

- The expressions on people's faces, their gestures and their posture can reveal more than what they say.
- We can learn to 'read' expressions, gestures and posture, for example, crossed arms and eyes averted can indicate defensive behaviour, smiles and eye contact can indicate open confidence.
- By learning to have some control over body language, people can avoid giving others the wrong impression about their feelings and intentions.

USING THE ACTIVITY SHEET

The focus of the activity is to develop pupils' awareness of their own body language and the ways in which other people respond to it.

Step 1 Tell the class that the purpose of the lesson is to examine body language – the expressions on people's faces, the gestures they make with their hands and their posture – to understand its effects on others and to learn to take some control over it. Point out that this is not to suggest that people should use body language to try to deceive other people.

Step 2 Give each group a collection of pictures of, or describe, people with different facial expressions, gestures and posture and ask them to discuss how relaxed, confident and happy each person is, whether they trust him or her and what else they can tell about him or her. Ask them to explain their answers.

Step 3 Show the pupils a picture of, or describe, someone with a tense, rigid facial expression, and ask them to describe the person's feelings. Point out that what might appear as sadness, anger or disapproval might really be tension or nervousness, and discuss how it is useful to try to relax the face so as to avoid giving others the wrong impression. Ask the pupils to complete the activity sheet, bearing in mind different interpretations of each facial expression, gesture or posture.

Step 4 Invite feedback from the pupils and discuss any different interpretations of each picture. Ask them to contribute to a list of positive actions that people could take to avoid giving the wrong impression if they feel nervous or anxious.

Extension Activities

- The pupils could watch sections from television 'soaps', make notes about the characters' body language, under the headings 'Facial expressions', 'Gestures' and 'Posture', and say what each character's body language expresses.

Outcomes

- Understanding how body language expresses feelings and how it can be misread.
- Becoming aware of the ways in which the pupils' feelings affect their facial expressions, gestures and posture.

Activity Sheet 6

Body language

1. Would you like to work with these people? Write ✔ or ✗ in the boxes next to the pictures. Write your reasons below.

a. 　b. 　c.

a. _____

b. _____

c. _____

2. Look at the pictures below. Are these people telling the truth? Write ✔ or ✗ in the boxes. How can you tell? Write your reasons below.

a. 　b. 　c.

a. _____

b. _____

c. _____

3. On the back of this page, make an annotated drawing, or write a description, of a group of three people: make one of them appear to be listening carefully to the others, one appear as if he or she is rejecting what the others are saying and one appear to be leading the discussion.

Activity 7 – Teacher's notes

Face, hands and body

Using body language to counteract feelings of nervousness or inadequacy

AIM

To develop pupils' ability to use body language to generate positive feelings.

Teaching Points

Optional materials
Pictures (for example, from magazines or newspapers) of people looking nervous, intimidated or as if they lack confidence.

- People can learn to use facial expressions, gestures and posture to create a feeling of confidence.
- By learning to have some control over facial expressions, gestures and posture, people can overcome negative feelings; for example, people who feel insecure in a situation tend to hunch their shoulders, look downwards and generally make themselves appear small, whereas confident people stand or sit up straight, smile and look at other people's faces.
- Self-confidence can be boosted by relaxing the shoulders, holding up the head, looking at people and smiling (or at least relaxing the facial muscles).

USING THE ACTIVITY SHEET

The focus of the activity is to develop pupils' awareness of the ways in which they can use body language to overcome feelings of nervousness and boost their own confidence in difficult situations.

Step 1 Tell the class that the purpose of the lesson is to learn how to use body language positively. Point out that this is not to suggest that people should use body language to try to deceive other people.

Step 2 Give each group one of the magazine pictures or describe a person's features (see Teaching Points) and ask the pupils to describe the person's feelings. Ask them what might be causing those feelings. Point out that it is very difficult to change the feelings that we experience in particular situations, but that it is easier to tackle the physical symptoms of feelings such as anxiety by concentrating on, say, breathing slowly and calmly or on relaxing a group of muscles: for example, the muscles in the face or hands.

Step 3 Invite pupils to enact the process of tensing and relaxing the groups of muscles they have identified. Ask them to describe how they feel when their muscles are tense and when they are relaxed. Invite the others to observe and to describe the 'messages' given by their body language. Ask the pupils to complete the activity sheet.

Step 4 With the class, make a list of 'Positive steps to take when you do not feel confident'.

Extension Activities

- The pupils could write leaflets to help younger pupils to feel confident in situations they find challenging.
- Ask the pupils to observe people on television who appear confident and to make notes of what they do that creates this impression.

Outcomes

- Using body language to help to overcome feelings of inadequacy, nervousness or anxiety.
- Developing ways of improving self-confidence by beginning to take control of a difficult situation.

Activity Sheet 7

Face, hands and body

1. Describe the body language of each of these people and what it tells you about their confidence (or lack of it).

The body language of **a** indicates

_____

_____

The body language of **b** indicates

_____

_____

The body language of **c** indicates

_____

_____

2. Which person looks the least confident? _____

3. Write some advice to this person to help her to tackle this lack of confidence by concentrating on facial expression, gestures and posture:

_____

_____

_____

_____

© Folens (copiable page)   ACTIVITY BANK: *Self-Esteem*   17

Activity 8 – Teacher's notes

Your values

We all have values that influence what we do

AIM

To encourage pupils to make explicit their own values and to respect the values of other people.

Teaching Points

- A value is what we feel is right, good or important. Examples include loyalty to friends, care for others or for the environment. Other values include those that we place on things: for example, items of sentimental value.
- Some values are shared by almost everyone (for example, that it is wrong to kill people or steal), whereas others might be shared by groups of people, communities, faith groups or individuals.
- We feel good when we act according to our values, but it is not always easy to do so.
- When people act according to their values their actions are not necessarily carried out for personal gain.

USING THE ACTIVITY SHEET

The focus of the activity is to develop pupils' understanding of their own values and to consider whether, and how, they can act according to them.

Step 1 Tell the class that the purpose of the lesson is to consider what we mean by values. Ask pupils to complete the activity sheet and then to share their responses with a partner.

Step 2 Invite feedback from the class, if there is an atmosphere of sufficient trust, and ask the pupils to say what the responses tell them about one another's values. List examples of values, such as success, honesty, sincerity, wealth, friendship, care or image. Discuss any conflicting values. Or you could offer some of your own responses and ask the class what they show about your values. Do they agree with them? Point out that we are entitled to have different values, and encourage the pupils to express (with respect) any disagreement they might feel.

Step 3 Ask the pupils to write down the three values which they think most people hold; record them on an overhead transparency, chalkboard or wipe-off board. Keep a tally of the number of times any values are repeated.

Step 4 Ask the pupils to write sentences about three values that they think are important. They need not share their list if they prefer not to; it could be kept for personal reference when making decisions about what to do.

Extension Activities

- The pupils could collaborate on a class list of shared values.
- Pupils could research the values that underpin different religions and make a display about them.

Outcomes

- Awareness of the pupils' own values.
- Respect for the values of other people.

Activity Sheet 8

Your values

If we all had to escape from the Earth to another planet, but could take only three things with us, what would you take, and why would you choose these things?

Write your choices in the spaceship. Around the spaceship write your reasons.

Activity 9 – Teacher's notes

Values and actions
Acting according to our values

AIM
To develop pupils' appreciation that acting according to their values engenders feelings of self-worth.

Teaching Points

- The pupils should first have completed Activity 8 and understood what is meant by 'values'. They should have articulated their own values and understood that some values are shared by almost everyone, whereas others are shared by groups of people, communities and individuals.
- We feel good when we behave according to our values and not so good when we do not, but it is not always easy to stick to our values.
- When people behave according to their values their actions are not necessarily carried out for personal gain.
- There might be a conflict between values and actions: for example, people who value the lives of animals might nonetheless use fly-killers in their kitchens in order to avoid food poisoning.

USING THE ACTIVITY SHEET

The focus of the activity is to encourage pupils to consider the extent to which they can act according to their values, and how doing so can increase their feelings of self-worth.

Step 1 Tell the class that the purpose of the lesson is to consider the match or mismatch between people's values and their actions, and for them to reflect on how far they can act according to their own values, and how doing so can increase their feelings of self-worth. Ask the pupils to give examples of some commonly held values. Focus on about six of these and then ask the class how each would affect the behaviour of the people who held them. An example might be, someone who believes that it is wrong to cause suffering to animals and decides to become a vegetarian.

Step 2 Tell the pupils that the activity sheet asks them to consider the effects of values on people's behaviour. Ask them to complete the activity sheet.

Step 3 Invite the pupils to share their responses to the activity sheet. Discuss the reasons why people do not always behave according to their values. These might be simple (for example, because it is easier or more tempting not to do so), or more complex (for example, because to do so might lead to confrontation). One example might be that of a man who says that women and men are equal, but expects a woman to give up work to care for a baby, cook and do housework. Another would be parents who say that children should always tell the truth, but then complain when their child embarrasses them by telling an uncomfortable truth.

Step 4 As an individual exercise, not necessarily to be shared with anyone else, ask the pupils to reflect on times when they have or have not acted according to their values. Ask them to record how they felt.

Extension Activities

- The pupils could use various texts (including newspaper reports) to research what happens when people's actions contravene the agreed values of a group or community. This could make the distinction between implicit and explicit agreements about values.

Outcomes

- Developing an understanding of the effects of people's values on the pupils' behaviour.
- Developing an awareness of how acting according to their values can increase the pupils' feelings of self-worth.

Activity Sheet 9

Values and actions

1. Read Becky and Liam's statements about their values. Write three sentences about what they would each do if they behaved according to their values. Write three sentences about what they would not do.

Becky

It is wrong to waste any materials.

It is important always to keep secret anything that I am told in confidence.

Liam

a. I would ...

_____

_____

_____

I would not ...

_____

_____

_____

b. I would ...

_____

_____

_____

I would not ...

_____

_____

_____

2. Describe a situation in which Liam and Becky might not behave according to their values. Explain what might cause this:

Liam _____

_____

_____

_____

Becky _____

_____

_____

_____

© Folens (copiable page) ACTIVITY BANK: *Self-Esteem*

Activity 10 – Teacher's notes

Feedback

Giving and accepting praise and criticism

AIM

To develop pupils' capacity to give praise and criticism and to accept them from others.

Teaching Points

- Other people can help us to appreciate our strengths and weaknesses.
- People find criticism easier to accept if they first have their positive points acknowledged and praised.
- Friends can help one another by offering praise and criticism.
- Praise and criticism are helpful when they are supported by examples of behaviour, rather than expressed as descriptive 'labels': for example, 'Sometimes you do things that stop people from trusting you, like when you told … what I had told you in confidence', rather than 'You are untrustworthy'.
- It is important to express criticism tactfully and in a way that shows understanding and wanting to help the person.

USING THE ACTIVITY SHEET

The focus of the activity is to encourage the pupils to identify the effects of their behaviour on the ways in which other people respond to them.

Step 1   Tell the class that the purpose of the lesson is to help them to accept praise for the things they do well and to accept, and act on, criticism that is designed to help them. They will also learn how they can support their friends in this process. Tell them that they are going to begin by making notes about what they can praise in a friend before they decide what they will say to him or her. You could model different ways of expressing praise and ask them which they prefer and why.

Step 2   Ask the pupils to complete the first 'speech bubble'. After they have done so, invite them to read out their responses or ask them to look for any that are descriptive (for example, 'You are artistic' or 'You are kind') and encourage them to express the responses using verbs rather than adjectives: for example, 'You draw brilliant portraits' or 'You show kindness when people are in trouble'.

Step 3   Ask the pupils to complete the second 'speech bubble' (using verbs rather than adjectives) and to discuss with a friend what they have written.

Step 4   Discuss how expressing praise and criticism in terms of actions is more helpful than giving people labels: people tend to live up to labels, whereas actions lead to personal development.

Extension Activities

- The pupils could make a personal log-book of the things for which they have been praised, to refer to whenever they have to do something in which they do not feel confident. Point out that they can remind themselves of the strengths that will help them in a particular situation.
- Help the pupils to use their friends' criticisms as starting points for setting achievable targets.

Outcomes

- Affirmation of abilities and areas needing to be developed.
- Developing the ability to accept praise and criticism.
- Developing skills in expressing praise and criticism in ways that are acceptable to the recipient.

Activity Sheet 10

Feedback

Nadine is very popular with her classmates. She's fun to be with and is always at the centre of things. Sometimes she forgets that other people are different.

Jake is very good at football and spends most of his spare time in training. He doesn't have much time for anything else.

1. Choose one of the characters above to be your friend. Around the speech bubble, make notes about anything you can praise in your friend. In the speech bubble, write what you will say to him or her.

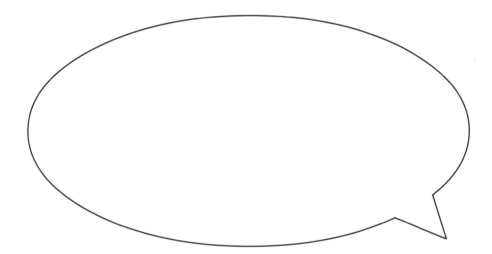

2. Around the speech bubble, make notes about anything you can criticise in your friend that will help him or her. In the speech bubble, write what you will say to him or her.

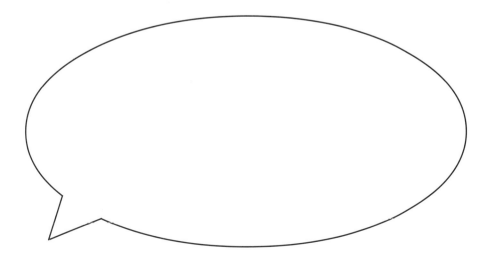

© Folens (copiable page)   ACTIVITY BANK: *Self-Esteem*

Activity 11 – Teacher's notes

Not again!

Learning from experience

AIM

To develop pupils' capacity to bring to mind previous experiences and to apply what they have learned from them to new situations.

Teaching Points

- People can learn from both positive and negative experiences.
- It is helpful for people to bear in mind the times when they got things right, to congratulate themselves and to remember what was right and why.
- Everyone makes mistakes, and it can be helpful to remember them in order to avoid making them again.
- It is natural for people to be ashamed of some of their mistakes and to want to forget them, but they can be turned into positive experiences for learning.
- The first stage in learning from mistakes is to admit to them. To be able to do so is a sign of confidence.

USING THE ACTIVITY SHEET

The focus of the activity is to encourage pupils to develop skills in thinking logically about experiences and applying what they have learned to new situations.

Step 1 Tell the class that the purpose of the lesson is to develop skills in learning from experiences (both positive and negative). Ask the pupils to write a short account of an experience in which they think they did the right thing and one in which they did the wrong thing. The accounts should be anonymous. Limit the number of words to 150 so that accounts can be pasted on to a postcard, or the pupils could word-process them and print them in a postcard-sized format. Alternatively, choose one or several of the accounts given on the activity sheet and give out to the pupils.

Step 2 Split the class into groups of about four and distribute the accounts. Ask the pupils to discuss them in their groups and to make notes about what could be learned from each experience.

Step 3 Invite feedback from each group. What might the person do the next time he or she faces a similar situation, and why?

Extension Activities

- The pupils could draw flow charts describing a situation, the various options for action in that situation, and what the outcome of each action might be.
- The pupils could role-play one of the case studies on the activity sheet, exploring both positive and negative endings.

Outcomes

- Developing the self-confidence to admit mistakes.
- Developing skills in making decisions and choices based on previous experiences.

Activity Sheet 11

Not again!

Positive case studies

Leroy found it really hard to make new friends and was a bit of a loner at school. Things seemed to get harder as he got older and many of his classmates were going to parties and meeting up after school. Then someone asked him whether he would like to join the local drama club. He'd always been interested in drama and although he was really nervous, he decided to go along. It was really difficult at first but after a while he gained confidence and started to make friends. Now he no longer feels left out of the group.

Stuart lived next door to an elderly neighbour, Bill, who couldn't get out much and didn't seem to have time for anyone. All the other neighbours said Bill was miserable and deserved to be sitting at home alone all day. One day a parcel was delivered to Stuart's house with Bill's name at the top. Stuart's mum asked him to take it next door so he went, hoping not to see his neighbour. When he got to the door Bill was standing there and invited him in for a chat. It turned out that Bill had once been a great cricketer. He began to show Stuart some key techniques. Now they get on really well together.

Becky had always been untidy at home and hated doing anything her mother told her to – thinking she was just being given a hard time. Then one day her mum walked out, crying, saying everyone took her for granted. Becky hadn't realised how her mum felt, so she tidied her room and even cleaned the kitchen before her mother got back. Since then they have been much closer.

Negative case studies

Daniel was two years older than his sister Jo and always felt she was too young and stupid to talk to. He never played with her or spoke to her friends when they came around to their place, although Jo really looked up to him. Then when he was 18 he went to a party and he saw his little sister across the room talking and laughing with some of his friends and it stopped him in his tracks.

Since she was thirteen, **Nadine** had never been interested in school work. She was far more interested in going out and didn't want to miss out on seeing friends. Then when she was sixteen she decided she wanted to become a doctor and would need to get good grades in order to go to university. Her teachers told her it might be too late.

When **Gemma** was 15 the group of friends she was with started bullying some of the other girls in her class. At first she thought it was funny and didn't believe it did anyone any real harm. After a while it became more serious and she could see that some of the victims were getting hurt or upset. She wanted to leave the group but they threatened to bully her if she did.

Activity 12 – Teacher's notes

Taking charge

Taking responsibility for organising schoolwork

AIM

To encourage pupils to take responsibility for organising their own work schedule.

Teaching Points

- The pupils should realise that when they make excuses (even if there is some truth in them) for not getting things done and maintain that they cannot do anything about it, they are taking a negative approach.
- On the other hand, when they accept responsibility, they are in control and can do something about the obstacles that hamper them.

USING THE ACTIVITY SHEET

The purpose of the activity is to encourage pupils to think logically about anything that stops them carrying out a task.

Step 1 Ask the class about any tasks (which may or may not be connected with school) that they have put off for any reason. In pairs, they could list the reasons they delayed completing, or even getting started on, a task.

Step 2 Invite the pupils to share the results of their discussions. Record their responses in separate lists (without writing the headings): difficulty, lack of time, distractions, pressure from others, poor preparation (disorganised files, lost notes, lost or broken equipment, no pen or pencil), disorganised working conditions. Ask the pupils to give a heading to each list. Invite them to identify the obstacles over which they have any control. In groups, they could discuss the actions they could have taken and the differences each might have made. Invite feedback.

Step 3 Ask the pupils to complete the activity sheet. Before writing the advice to Natalie, they should think about which obstacles she can control, and how. What else, over which she has no control, might have stopped her doing her revision and what could she do? Discuss who could help, and how. Discuss the feelings Natalie might have had in the situation portrayed in the picture. Compare these feelings with those she might have had after following some of the advice. What might have altered her feelings?

Step 4 Review the activity by highlighting the key points: the pupils can take control of tasks they have to carry out by organising their work and by seeking help when necessary.

Extension Activities

- The pupils could word-process a set of 'Tips for revision' to display in the classroom.
- Role-play what might happen to a) someone who continually makes excuses for not carrying out tasks, and b) someone who tackles the obstacles that are stopping him or her carrying out tasks.

Outcomes

- Developing a positive attitude towards taking responsibility for tasks.
- Developing positive feelings as a result of taking control of a situation.

Activity Sheet 12

Taking charge

1. Natalie cannot get started on her exam revision. What is stopping her?

   _____
   _____
   _____
   _____
   _____
   _____
   _____
   _____
   _____
   _____
   _____
   _____

2. How can Natalie help herself? Write a note giving her some suggestions.

   Dear Natalie,

Activity 13 – Teacher's notes

On the surface?

Taking care of one's appearance can increase self-respect

AIM

To examine the ways in which taking care of their appearance can increase the pupils' self-respect.

Teaching Points

Optional materials
A collection of photographs (from clothing catalogues, newspapers and magazines) of young adults wearing different types of clothes and with different hairstyles, and pictures of other adults (of all ages) dressed differently. Include some smartly dressed people, some sporty and some looking unkempt in each set of pictures.

- People have different ideas about how they like to look. These might have a cultural or religious basis.
- Most people feel better when they have taken care over their appearance.
- A person's appearance can influence the ways in which other people respond to him or her.

USING THE ACTIVITY SHEET

The focus of the activity is to examine the ways in which the pupils' appearance affects both the way they feel and how other people respond to them.

Step 1   Tell the pupils that the purpose of the activity is to examine how appearance can affect our feelings about ourselves, and the way in which others respond to us. Ask the pupils if they think a person's appearance matters.

Step 2   Split the class into groups. Tell the groups that they must decide on and make a list of aspects of someone's appearance they would take into account when choosing a) a person they would want to socialise with, and b) a person they would trust to be their doctor. If you have them, give out photographs to help their decisions. Ask them to justify their choices to the class.

Step 3   Ask the pupils to complete the activity sheet.

Step 4   Invite the pupils to share their responses to the activity. Discuss the reasons behind their answers; to what extent were they influenced by fashion, by what their friends wear or by the considerations of their religion? Ask them how they think they should present themselves for situations such as an interview for a job or meeting friends for an evening.

Extension Activities

- Discuss how the pupils would dress for going to a church, mosque, synagogue or temple and investigate the influence of religion on clothing and other aspects of appearance.
- Explore the way in which a person's appearance shows respect for other people. Discuss how the pupils would dress when doing work experience, for example, in an office or a bank.

Outcomes

- Developing an understanding of the effects of appearance on self-respect.
- Developing an appreciation of the ways in which someone's appearance affects other people.

Activity Sheet 13

On the surface?

1. Make an annotated drawing of how you like to look. Explain how you feel when you look your best.

When I look my best _____
_____
_____
_____
_____
_____
_____
_____
_____
_____
_____

2. Make another annotated drawing of yourself. This time show how you would not want to appear when in front of your friends. Explain how you would feel.

When I don't look my best _____
_____
_____
_____
_____
_____
_____
_____
_____
_____
_____
_____

Activity 14 – Teacher's notes

No panic!

Keeping calm under pressure

AIM

To develop pupils' capacity to cope with pressure.

Teaching Points

Optional materials
A diary or calendar for each pupil. The pupils could produce these for themselves before the lesson, using a word-processor.

- Short, achievable tasks are easier to face than long ones. We feel a sense of achievement on completing a task.
- Coursework and exam revision are easier to complete if the pupils approach them in stages and record each stage as a completed task. This could be linked with target-setting.
- The pupils will feel a greater sense of achievement if they can organise their work for themselves (albeit with the support of a friend or teacher) than if someone else does it for them.

USING THE ACTIVITY SHEET

The focus of the activity is on recognising that having many things to do can be stressful, and on developing organisational methods to manage such tasks.

Step 1 Ask pupils to think about any events in history, plays, films or books that would have been completely different had key events not been delayed. For example, if Henry VIII's first wife had produced a son, or if Juliet's message to Romeo had not arrived too late, so that he believed her dead. Split the class into groups and ask them to list any tasks they have put off during the past month and any tasks that they did as soon as they could.

Step 2 Compare the lists. Are there any similarities between the tasks that were put off? Discuss the reasons. Compare these with the tasks they did not put off. Did they put off those that required a great deal of effort or time, or that were boring or difficult?

Step 3 Ask the pupils how they felt when other people (for example, parents, carers or teachers) reminded them of outstanding work – did they feel as if they were being nagged? How did they react? Ask them about their feelings about tasks they knew they must do but had not begun, such as homework or exam revision. Discuss the ways in which the pupils have coped with pressure. Did they make excuses or even stay away from school to avoid the consequences?

Step 4 Ask the pupils to complete the activity sheet. Help them to be realistic about the time each task will take by comparing it with other similar tasks they have done. Discuss the benefits of breaking down a large task into smaller ones: it helps to make a task achievable, and success is experienced as each part is completed. Suggest that the pupils organise their work with a friend as supporter and mentor.

Extension Activities

- Help the pupils to use the process introduced in the activity to plan their exam revision. Suggest also that they intersperse topics they dislike or find difficult with those they enjoy or find easy.

Outcomes

- Developing practical strategies for coping with pressure.
- Pupils taking responsibility for their own learning.

Activity Sheet 14

No panic!

Sometimes you have so much to do that you put off getting started on it. That gives you even less time in which to do it. You need a calendar or diary.

1. List the things you have to do. Next to each item on the list, write a deadline date.
2. Complete the chart on the right to show how long each task will take.

Task	Deadline

Time	Tasks
Less than 30 minutes	
30 minutes to 1 hour	
1 to 3 hours*	
More than 3 hours*	

* Find a way to split these into shorter tasks.

3. Prioritise each task with a number:
    1 – urgent
    2 – in the next two days
    3 – in the next week
4. On a calendar, in a diary, or on the back of this sheet, write when you will start and finish each task.

© Folens (copiable page) ACTIVITY BANK: *Self-Esteem*

Activity 15 – Teacher's notes

Getting angry

Managing anger

AIM

To develop pupils' ability to cope with anger.

Teaching Points

- Some people become angry more easily than others.
- If people act in ways that are out of control when they are angry (for example, by shouting, withdrawing socially, being aggressive or even becoming physically ill), they need help in dealing with the emotion.
- Research (see BBC Mental Health website: www.bbc.co.uk/health/mental/anger.shtml) has found that expressing anger in uncontrolled ways can increase it rather than calm the person, because it does not resolve the situation.
- To deal with anger, people need to recognise the causes of it and to develop strategies for coping with it. They cannot always avoid the events or people that cause their anger but they can take control either by making changes to situations, or by changing the way in which they react to them.

USING THE ACTIVITY SHEET

The focus of the activity is on how to express anger in socially acceptable ways and how to control it.

Step 1 Tell the pupils that the purpose of the lesson is to explore how to stay in control when they are angry. Ask them to picture people they have observed expressing anger. What caused the anger and how did they express it? List the pupils' responses. What might happen the next time these people are in a similar situation? It is likely that they would respond in the same way. Have they gained anything through their anger? Point out that they were being controlled by the people or events which caused their anger.

Step 2 Ask the pupils to complete the first part of the activity sheet, basing their responses on one of the situations discussed.

Step 3 Discuss with pupils ways of controlling anger. For example:
- through relaxation techniques such as breathing slowly and deeply from the diaphragm (you could practise this in class), repeating a calming word such as 'relax' or visualising a relaxing experience
- through logic: for example, reasoning that a parent does not get up in the morning and decide to make your life a misery.

Pupils can use this discussion to help them answer the second part of the activity.

Step 4 Explore ways of expressing anger so that whoever caused it can understand how and why, and the situation can be resolved. Review what has been learned, emphasising that, in managing anger, people can take control of a situation rather than letting it control them.

Extension Activities

- The pupils could research techniques of coping with anger and practise those that they find helpful.
- Organise role-play activities in which anger is expressed in socially acceptable ways that help to resolve the situation that caused it.

Outcomes

- Developing practical strategies for coping with anger.
- Recognising that it is normal to feel anger, but that losing control does not help.

Activity Sheet 15

Getting angry

1a. Inside the body outline, write words to describe the physical feelings of anger.

2b. Around the outline write what the person might do if he or she cannot control the feeling of anger.

2a. Inside the body outline write words to describe the physical sensations of the angry person who is using methods of coping with that anger.

2b. Around the outline, write what he or she can do to stay in control.

Teachers' notes *(mask before photocopying)*
If pupils find using words too difficult, the activity can be modified by using different colours to indicate feelings of anger.

Activity 16 – Teacher's notes

Feeling and thinking

Understanding interactions between emotions and thought

AIM

To develop pupils' ability to recognise emotions and deal with them through focusing on their thoughts.

Teaching Points

Optional materials
A video recording of a television drama or 'soap' in which someone's emotions affect his or her reactions to a situation; a television set and video player.

- It can be difficult to control emotions; thoughts are easier to control.
- Emotions affect the ways in which people respond to situations; on the other hand, situations can trigger emotions. By focusing on thoughts, people can take some control of their emotional reactions.
- Pupils who frequently experience extreme emotions should be offered counselling, according to the school's policies for support. Specialist support should be sought if necessary.

USING THE ACTIVITY SHEET

The focus of the activity is on identifying the ways in which emotions affect thoughts, making the most of positive emotions and using thoughts to cope with negative ones.

Step 1 Tell the pupils that the purpose of the lesson is to help them to develop strategies for dealing with uncomfortable emotions such as anxiety, fear and sadness. Describe a scene or play a video recording of part of a television drama in which someone's emotions affect his or her reactions to a situation. One example might be the scene from *EastEnders* where Lisa shot Phil Mitchell because he was abusive and unfaithful. Ask the pupils to suggest other ways in which the person could have responded and to decide which would have been the best.

Step 2 Ask the pupils to complete the activity sheet. Invite feedback, and discuss any differences between their responses.

Step 3 Discuss other situations in which the pupils might find themselves, and ask them about the different ways in which they might respond to them. Which responses would make them feel good?

Step 4 Split the pupils into groups and ask them to role-play some of the situations they have described, enacting the responses that create positive feelings. Point out that practising responses to situations in which the pupils feel uncomfortable prepares them for real-life situations.

Extension Activities

- The pupils could produce leaflets to help younger children to use thoughts to cope with emotions such as fear and anxiety in situations common to their age group.
- Encourage the pupils to keep an 'emotions diary' in which they record the emotions they feel each day, the situations that trigger them (or those that have no apparent cause) and how they behave in response to them.

Outcomes

- Understanding the effects of emotions on behaviour.
- Developing practical strategies for coping with negative emotions.

Activity Sheet 16

Feeling and thinking

Write what someone might think in each situation, depending on his or her emotions at the time:

Situation	Happy	Unhappy	Anxious
A friend does not call when he or she promised to.			
Arriving somewhere before any friends and not knowing anyone there.			
Not being chosen for a school team or a part in a play.			
Seeing someone he or she knows on the bus but the person does not say 'Hello'.			
Not receiving a birthday card by someone who usually sends one.			

© Folens (copiable page) ACTIVITY BANK: Self-Esteem 35

Activity 17 – Teacher's notes

Stressed out

Recognising stress

AIM

To help the pupils to recognise stress and to understand what causes it.

Teaching Points

- Stress is a normal reaction to difficult situations. The more difficult or risky the situation, the more extreme are the physical manifestations of stress caused by the release of the hormone adrenalin: an increase in heartbeat, higher blood-pressure and breathing rate.
- Physical activity uses the extra adrenalin in the body.
- Normal stress is useful in preparing the body to react to a risky situation.
- Excess stress causes health problems: emotional, rather than physical, stress does not use up the extra adrenalin in the body.
- People cannot control all the causes of stress, but they can take responsibility for coping with them. Pupils having difficulty coping with stress should be offered counselling according to the school's policies, and specialist help should be sought if necessary.

USING THE ACTIVITY SHEET

The focus of the activity is on understanding what stress is, how to recognise it and how it is caused.

Step 1 Tell the pupils that the purpose of the lesson is to develop their understanding of stress, and how to recognise it and its causes. Ask them to complete the activity sheet, which will help them to find out how much they already know about stress and about any misunderstandings they may have.

Step 2 Invite feedback from the pupils about the causes of stress. Write on the board any common causes they have omitted, to add to their activity sheet. Examples are death of a loved one, injury or illness, divorce in the family, problems in relationships or friendships, pressure from other people, exams, moving house or other changes in home circumstances, change of school, and breaking the law. Even holidays and festivals can cause stress through change of normal routine.

Step 3 Discuss any causes of stress over which the pupils can have any control, and how.

Step 4 Discuss the symptoms of stress and tell the pupils about the normal physical sensations of stress in a difficult situation (see Teaching Points). List any others that the pupils have omitted, to add to their activity sheets. Examples might be tiredness, fear, irritation, depression, tearfulness and anxiety. Physical symptoms might include headaches, digestive problems and panic attacks in which the sufferer might experience palpitations (abnormal heartbeat), breath 'catching' in the throat, a tight feeling in the chest, hyperventilation (rapid or very deep breathing), dizziness, cold sweats, nausea and ringing in the ears. People suffering from extreme stress might harm themselves. Ensure that the pupils know what support for coping with stress is available from the school and other organisations (see Activity 22).

Extension Activities

- The pupils could produce computer-generated checklists for working out how susceptible they are to stress according to the known causes. They could also make 'symptoms checklists'.

Outcomes

- Recognising the causes and symptoms of stress.
- Developing an understanding of normal and excessive levels of stress.

Activity Sheet 17

Stressed out

1. In the arrows write anything you can think of that causes stress.
2. In the body outline write all the physical symptoms of stress.

Teachers' notes *(mask before photocopying)*
If pupils find using words too difficult, they could use different colours to indicate feelings and levels of stress.

© Folens (copiable page)   ACTIVITY BANK: *Self-Esteem*

Activity 18 – Teacher's notes

Stress busters

Coping with stress

AIM

To help pupils to cope with stress from different causes.

Teaching Points

- The pupils should first have completed Activity 17.
- People can take positive steps to control stress. Pupils having difficulty coping with stress should be offered counselling according to the school's policies, and specialist help should be sought if necessary.
- General coping strategies for stress can be developed.
- Sometimes the causes of stress can be controlled.
- Sometimes the symptoms of stress need to be tackled first: for example, headaches.

USING THE ACTIVITY SHEET

The focus of the activity is on identifying what causes stress and working out ways to cope with it.

Step 1 Tell the pupils that the purpose of the lesson is to develop their ability to cope with stress. Point out that stress can be caused by everyday events as well as momentous ones such as death or divorce in the family, accidents or serious illnesses. Ask the pupils to name examples of everyday causes of stress (from Activity 17). Some might be missing the bus, sitting a school exam, or going to the dentist. Ask them to write each cause of stress on a separate card or piece of paper.

Step 2 Ask the pupils to complete the activity sheet. Make a blank copy of the grid, on which they can write other tips they have come across, including taking care of their health: eating well, getting enough sleep, relaxing and so on. Invite feedback.

Step 3 Discuss how the tips could help people suffering from stress: for example, 'Saying "no"' could include taking steps to avoid having too many demands made on them. It could be linked with 'Be assertive' – pointing out in a reasonable way to parents or others if they are asking too much and saying why; telling them how this causes stress and working out ways of avoiding it without conflict.

Step 4 Ask the pupils to cut out the tips for managing stress and to match them with the causes they wrote on cards at the beginning of the lesson. Ensure that they know what support for coping with stress is available from the school and from other organisations (see Activity 22).

Extension Activities

- Invite a stress counsellor to give a talk to the pupils.
- Using an example from the activity, pupils could role-play a stressful situation and show how it could be managed.

Outcomes

- Developing general coping strategies for stress.
- Encouraging a positive attitude towards managing stress.

Activity Sheet 18

Stress busters

1. Read the tips for reducing stress and write details of the practical ways in which you could follow them.

Try to compromise.	Be assertive.
Keep things in proportion.	Say 'no'.
Prepare.	Ask for help.
Don't take on other people's bad moods.	Let go of things that upset you.
Deal with your hurt feelings.	Do something every day that makes you feel good.

2. On the back of the sheet, draw a cartoon to illustrate one of your stress busters.

Activity 19 – Teacher's notes

Sad or depressed?

Understanding depression

AIMS

To help pupils to understand the difference between feeling unhappy and being depressed, and to know where to find help for depression.

Teaching Points

- It is normal to feel unhappy sometimes. This includes being miserable about something specific. Normal sadness can be forgotten during enjoyable activities; sufferers have an idea of what might make them feel better.
- The following are signs of a depressed person: feeling powerless, being uninterested in what is going on around them, feeling that life is not worth living, not knowing what is making them unhappy, being moody or irritable, not wanting to go out, crying a lot, eating a lot more or a lot less than usual, having bad dreams or trouble in sleeping, wanting to harm themselves (or actually doing so), a need for constant reassurance.
- The school's child protection and anti-bullying policies should be followed if abuse or bullying affect any of the pupils.
- See also Activity 22, which suggests ways in which the pupils can help one another and seek help if they have problems such as depression.

USING THE ACTIVITY SHEET

The focus of the activity is on how to recognise and cope with depression.

Step 1 Tell the pupils that the purpose of the lesson is to develop their understanding of depression and how to cope with it. Point out that it is normal for people to feel unhappy sometimes, but that depression is much more serious. Discuss the use of the word 'depressed'; the pupils might have heard people saying they are 'depressed' (or even said it themselves) when what they really mean is that they feel fed up or unhappy about something.

Step 2 Split the pupils into groups and ask them to compile a list of possible causes of depression. Invite feedback and record their responses. If they have not mentioned the following you could add them to the list: the same causes as those for stress (see Activity 17); worrying about looks, sexuality, or a parent or carer who is depressed; feeling worthless or isolated; being bullied or abused.

Step 3 Ask the pupils to complete the activity sheet. Invite them to share their responses; discuss any differences in their answers, and tell them some of the recognised signs of depression (see Teaching Points).

Step 4 Discuss the ways in which people can tell if they are suffering from depression and how it might help if they keep an 'emotions diary' in which they record how they feel at different times. If there are times when they feel happy and relaxed it is unlikely that they are suffering from depression.

Extension Activities

- The pupils could research the symptoms of depression and compile checklists – 'Depressed or unhappy?'
- They could write for information from organisations that offer advice about stress (see Activity 22) and write leaflets or instructions on how to help a friend who is depressed.

Outcomes

- Ability to recognise the signs of depression and to distinguish it from feeling unhappy or fed up.
- Developing an understanding of the causes of depression.

Activity Sheet 19

Sad or depressed?

Are these people depressed or are they just feeling unhappy or fed up?
Explain your answers.

I'm upset about my parents. They were shouting at one another for ages. Dad had used Mum's car and left it without petrol. She was furious. When she stopped for breath – and it wasn't often (she can go for ages without oxygen; she'd be a brilliant underwater swimmer) – he pointed out that she often did the same with his car. I hope they don't get divorced.

She has lost a lot of weight. She hardly eats. She always used to work hard but now she finds it hard to concentrate and is getting behind with her work.

They wait for me every day after school. I'm not going today. I feel too ill. I'm staying in bed.

I can't have the trainers I want. I'm so depressed. Dad says they are too expensive, so I'll have to save up. It's not fair. He's got all the latest gear.

They laugh at my clothes and my hair. They say I'm ugly. I am ugly. I hate school. Mum ignores me. If I did something really bad she'd have to take notice. It wasn't quite so bad when Grandad was alive.

I really miss Jamila since she moved house. There's no one else I trust with my secrets. I'm looking forward to going to stay with her.

I hate being taller than all my friends. I'm not keen on my nickname ('String') either. I feel upset when they tease me. But I don't think they are trying to be mean.

© Folens (copiable page)   ACTIVITY BANK: *Self-Esteem*   41

Activity 20 – Teacher's notes

Danger – eating disorders

Information about eating disorders

AIM

To ensure that pupils have accurate information about eating disorders.

Teaching Points

Optional materials
Information texts about eating disorders, including magazine articles and leaflets.

- Anorexia nervosa is deliberate severe weight loss through starvation, exercise or vomiting. The sufferer has a morbid fear of being fat and an obsessive determination to be thin.
- Bulimia nervosa is characterised by binge eating (up to about 10 000 calories (40 000 joules) in a few hours), an obsession with weight loss and an absence of control over eating.
- The physical symptoms of anorexia nervosa are weight loss (more than 20% of normal body weight), constipation, a growth of hair on the body and face, feeling cold even in warm weather, poor sleep and (in girls) the stopping of periods.
- The physical symptoms of bulimia nervosa are not so noticeable: for example, calluses or abrasions on the backs of the fingers (caused by the teeth during induced vomiting). There is not always weight loss.
- Both anorexia and bulimia can cause severe damage in the long term. Anorexia can lead to osteoporosis, infertility, chronic depression and poor circulation and, if not cured, starvation and death. Bulimia can cause erosion of the teeth from stomach acids (they can be reduced to black stumps), irritation or inflammation and even ulceration of the gullet and lowering of the body's potassium levels through vomiting; this can cause an irregular heartbeat and even a heart attack.

USING THE ACTIVITY SHEET

The focus of the activity is on learning the facts about eating disorders, their symptoms and long-term effects.

Step 1 Tell the pupils that the purpose of the lesson is for them to learn about the physical and behavioural symptoms of eating disorders and their long-term effects and to clear up any misunderstandings they have.

Step 2 Ask the pupils to complete the first part of the activity sheet. Tell them the definitions of anorexia nervosa and bulimia nervosa. Discuss their responses and question any misconceptions they have.

Step 3 Tell the pupils the physical symptoms and long-term effects of eating disorders. Tell them about the behavioural symptoms of anorexia and bulimia (see also Activity 22). You could also provide magazine articles and other information texts for pupils to read.

Step 4 Ask the pupils to make notes about the symptoms and long-term effects of eating disorders and to organise the information they have collected, using the chart on the activity sheet.

Extension Activities

- Ask the pupils to make notes for, plan and write a report about how to spot if someone is suffering from an eating disorder, in order to help him or her.

Outcomes

- Developing knowledge and understanding of the physical and behavioural symptoms of anorexia and bulimia nervosa and their long-term effects.
- Recognising the seriousness of eating disorders.

Activity Sheet 20

Danger – eating disorders

1. On the notepads, write what you know about anorexia nervosa and bulimia nervosa.

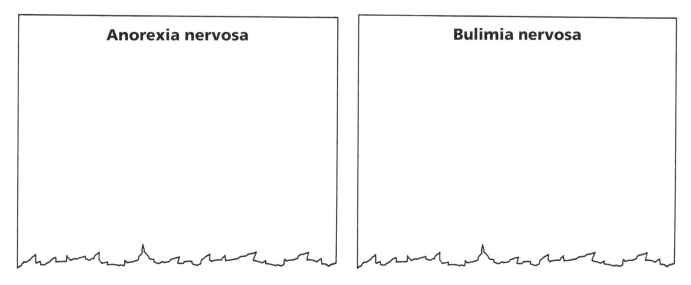

2. Use the chart to organise your notes about the effects of the illnesses.

Effects on:	Anorexia nervosa	Bulimia nervosa
bones		
circulation		
heart		
digestive system		
reproductive system		
skin		
overall appearance		
feelings		
private or secretive behaviour		
noticeable behaviour		

© Folens (copiable page)   ACTIVITY BANK: *Self-Esteem*

Activity 21 – Teacher's notes

Emotions and eating

The causes of eating disorders and how to avoid them

AIM

To develop pupils' awareness of how eating disorders begin and how to avoid them (and to help people close to them to do so).

Teaching Points

- The pupils should first have completed Activity 20.
- Anorexia nervosa and bulimia nervosa are illnesses and not merely extreme forms of dieting for weight loss.
- Both of these illnesses arise from emotional problems that underlie the sufferer's obsession with weight control: for example, low self-esteem, depression or stress.
- Although anorexia or bulimia can be triggered by an event, remark or idea (for example, wanting to be as slim as a friend, or a chance remark about their size), these are not the real causes, although frequent teasing about their weight could lead to depression.
- Many sufferers do not want to be cured even though the illness can kill them. At the time of writing, there are several websites (although access to them is blocked by some servers) created by sufferers to celebrate anorexia and to encourage other sufferers not to give in to pressure to change. Teachers might want to discuss why some people want to encourage others to be anorexic or bulimic.

USING THE ACTIVITY SHEET

The focus of the activity is on understanding the causes of eating disorders in order to avoid them and to help others who are affected.

Step 1 Tell the pupils that the purpose of the lesson is for them to learn about the causes of eating disorders, how to avoid them and how they can help anyone close to them who is affected by them.

Step 2 Ask the pupils to complete the first part of the activity sheet. Invite them to share their responses. Discuss these and challenge any assumptions: neither thin people nor people who are overweight are necessarily suffering from eating disorders. What is a 'normal' weight for some people might not be for others. If people diet to lose some weight it does not necessarily lead to anorexia. Can the pupils identify other factors that are more relevant?

Step 3 Revise what the pupils know about the factors that affect self-esteem and the causes of depression and stress. Ask them to discuss, in groups, how people can help themselves and one another to develop attitudes and feelings that avoid eating problems. Invite feedback and write on a board or overhead transparency the key points: care, sympathy, support, understanding, confidence, self-respect and self-worth.

Step 4 Ask the pupils to complete the second part of the activity sheet, focusing on actions they can take: for example, offering kind words when someone is upset or praising a friend's achievement.

Extension Activities

- The pupils could plan and write a class 'code of conduct' for supporting one another.
- They could prepare questions for a visiting speaker (if one can be arranged) about practical ways of helping people who are suffering from eating disorders or are having other problems that might lead to them.

Outcomes

- Developing knowledge and understanding of the causes of anorexia and bulimia nervosa.
- Developing appreciation of the role friends can play in affirming one another's self-esteem.
- Knowing how pupils can help anyone close to them who has developed an eating disorder.

Activity Sheet 21

Emotions and eating

1. Which of these people do you think might develop either anorexia nervosa or bulimia nervosa, and why?

a.
> I am a fat boy. My mum and dad are fat. We are all fat in my family. Maybe if we stopped eating chips we would get a bit thinner. I wouldn't want any of them to change too much, and I don't think they would want me to.

b.
> I weigh nine stone. That's about two stone more than models who are taller than me. If I could be as thin as they are I could look really good, then the other girls would respect me more.

c.
> I need to stay thin to be a good runner. Fat slows you down. The thinner I get the faster I can run. I am completely in control. People who are fat just have no control over their eating.

d.
> I like food. I like going for a pizza with my friends. Des said I am putting on weight. I probably am, but I'm growing taller, too.

a. _____

b. _____
_____

c. _____
_____

d. _____
_____

2. What can you do to help a friend who might be developing an eating disorder? Write your ideas on the back of this sheet.

Activity 22 – Teacher's notes

Help

Finding help in coping with stress, depression and eating disorders

AIM

To develop pupils' awareness of the sources of help that are available to them.

Teaching Points

Materials needed
The school's policies and procedures for pupil support, local directories, access to the Internet (or printouts of relevant material from the websites listed below).

- The pupils should first have completed as many as possible of the other activities in this book.
- The pupils should know which members of staff have responsibility for their support and welfare.
- Some pupils might prefer to talk about any problems to their doctor or to a counsellor they do not know.
- The following organisations can be helpful: CALM (Campaign Against Living Miserably) 0800 585858, Careline 020 8514 1177, Childline 0800 1111, Eating Disorders Association 01603 765050, MIND (National Association for Mental Health) 0345 660163, No Panic 01952 590545, The Samaritans 0345 678000, Young Minds 020 7336 8445.
- Useful websites include **www.mentalhealth.org.uk, www.youth2youth.co.uk, www.thesite.org, www.samaritans.org.uk**, and **www.mind.org.uk**.

Some pages or sites on the Internet may be unsuitable for pupils to view so care is needed. Their access can be limited by saving pages in advance to view offline, by providing restricted links or by using filtering software.

USING THE ACTIVITY SHEET

The focus of the activity is on considering the best ways to find help for specific problems.

Step 1 Tell the pupils that the purpose of the lesson is to ensure that they know how and where to find help for problems such as depression, stress and eating disorders, if they need it. Point out that no one goes through life without coming up against problems, but that some people cope with them better than others. Also point out that, as they have learned from other activities, the pupils can develop skills in coping.

Step 2 List the problems about which the pupils have learned (for example, stress, depression and eating disorders). Split the class into groups. Allocate a topic to each group and ask them to complete the first part of the activity sheet (their questions).

Step 3 Ask the pupils to exchange activity sheets with another group whose members write answers to the questions using the information available, and give their sources.

Step 4 Ask the pupils to return the activity sheets to the groups from which they came and then to evaluate the responses for sensitivity, relevance and usefulness, and for how effective they would be in helping to overcome a problem. Invite feedback from each group about the most useful ways to deal with each problem.

Extension Activities

- The pupils could compile 'Help' directories for specific problems, giving names (if appropriate), addresses, telephone numbers and website addresses along with evaluations.

Outcomes

- Knowing how and where to find help with problems connected with stress, depression and eating disorders.

Activity Sheet 22

Help

1. Under each of the headings below, write three questions that someone suffering from _____ might ask.

2. Pass this page on to another group to research the answers.

Questions	Answers	Sources
Information (facts)		
Support (who can help)		
Advice (practical things you can do)		

Skills matrix

ACTIVITY/SKILL	1	2	3	4	5	6	7	8	9	10	11	12	13	14	15	16	17	18	19	20	21	22
Analysing/Interpreting					●	●					●	●		●	●	●	●	●		●	●	●
Asserting	●	●					●															
Awareness	●	●	●	●	●	●	●	●	●	●	●	●	●	●	●	●	●	●	●	●	●	●
Collating																				●		●
Communicating			●	●	●	●	●	●			●	●				●	●					●
Comparing					●	●	●				●					●	●				●	●
Cooperating										●												
Debating and discussing	●				●					●									●		●	
Decision making												●		●								
Empathising					●	●				●									●		●	
Evaluating												●		●								●
Expressing (e.g. beliefs, ideas and opinions)					●			●	●	●						●	●					
ICT												●		●			●					●
Identity and self-esteem	●	●	●	●	●	●	●	●	●	●	●	●	●	●	●	●	●	●	●	●	●	●
Imagining							●		●	●												
Investigating																	●					●
Developing knowledge																	●	●	●	●	●	●
Listening		●		●	●					●									●		●	
Negotiating																		●				
Perceiving			●	●	●	●	●	●	●	●	●	●	●	●	●	●	●	●	●		●	
Presenting		●					●															
Prioritising												●		●								
Problem solving											●	●		●								●
Respect				●		●				●												
Responsibility													●	●								
Understanding	●			●	●	●			●	●	●					●	●	●	●	●	●	●